ART SPIRITS

poems by

Diane Solis

Finishing Line Press
Georgetown, Kentucky

ART SPIRITS

*To my brothers and our mother,
and to our father in memoriam.*

Copyright © 2018 by Diane Solis
ISBN 978-1-63534-483-7 First Edition
All rights reserved under International and Pan-American Copyright Conventions.
No part of this book may be reproduced in any manner whatsoever without written permission from the publisher, except in the case of brief quotations embodied in critical articles and reviews.

ACKNOWLEDGMENTS

The author gratefully acknowledges the editors and publishers of the following journals where these poems previously appeared:

America, the Jesuit Review, "Mantis"
Ardor Literary Magazine, "Bennies"
Avocet, a Journal of Nature Poems, "Dawn" ("Doe at Dawn")
The Healing Muse, Annual Journal of the Center for Ethics and Humanities, SUNY, "Lucky"
Label Me Latina/o, "Flying Dreams" ("My Father's Dreams of Flying")
Psychological Perspectives, Journal of the C.G. Jung Institute, Los Angeles, "Coyotl" (forthcoming)
Sinister Wisdom, "Gifted" and "Like Father, like Daughter" ("Chip on Her Shoulder")
Slink Chunk Press, "Dolphin Skeleton," "Super Hero," and "Tigers"

Publisher: Leah Maines
Editor: Christen Kincaid
Cover Art: Diane Solis
Author Photo: L.M. Brabo, PhD
Cover Design: Elizabeth Maines McCleavy

Printed in the USA on acid-free paper.
Order online: www.finishinglinepress.com
also available on amazon.com

Author inquiries and mail orders:
Finishing Line Press
P. O. Box 1626
Georgetown, Kentucky 40324
U. S. A.

Table of Contents

I. Working with What We Have
The Apprentice Butcher and the Slaughterhouse Workers 1
Pinkie and the Lions 2
Bar Tender 3
Young Ms. Torrez 4
Bennies 5
Beautiful Japanese Quails 6
Thirst like This 7

II. Sketches Near and Far
Tigers of Her Imagination, *Chiang Mai, Thailand* 8
Flying Dreams, *Maravilla, Los Angeles* 9
Dolphin Skeleton, *Kachemak Bay, Alaska* 10
Novice at the Cafe, *New Brunswick, Canada* 11
Red Baseball Cap, *Salem, Massachusetts* 12
Catchy Tune, *French Quarter, New Orleans* 13
Michael Callahan, Crab Fisherman, *County Kerry, Ireland* 14

III. Drawing from Inspiration
Dawn 15
Mantis 17
Coyotl 18
Peaches at the Side Yard 19
Golden 20
Cigarettes 21
Late in the Dawning 23

IV. Gaining Perspective
Lucky 24
Superhero 25
Gifted 26
Like Father, like Daughter 28
Before the Ecstasy 30
Petals 32
In Parting, for the Reader 33

An artist must first of all respond to his subject, he must be filled with emotion toward that subject and then he must make his technique so sincere, so translucent that it may be forgotten, the value of the subject shining through it.

Robert Henri, *The Art Spirit*

The poems in this collection have evolved from a habit of watching, studying, listening, intuiting, and wishing to honor the quality and value beneath and beyond the surface of things. While the underlying stories of subjects, including people, places, and animals depicted in these pages may or may not be fully known, the author attempts to capture soulful aspects of each unique presence in its world. Amalgams have been crafted in some instances, while details are changed in others to respect and protect everyone's privacy.

I. Working with What We Have

The Apprentice Butcher and the Slaughterhouse Workers

Age fourteen, the apprentice butcher grabs a bucket
and hurries to the slaughterhouse. His first errand.
In a dull light there, the largest men stand under
the most gargantuan bulls that hang upside down

and dead, or nearly. The bulls' muscles ripple,
nerves firing and throbbing, limbs twitching,
legs still kicking, while the men hold filthy cups
to catch blood from fountains spouting out

of deep slashes in the animals' throats. Jostling
for turns, workers fill their cups to guzzle the serum
hot from the dead and dying. "What do you want?"
a goliath snarls, wiping his blood-spattered face

neck, and chest, nodding towards the pails brimming
with skinless tails over in a corner near the door.
The boy trades his bucket for a full one and pivots
to leave. "You missed one!" Hercules barks, handing

him an extra, with a grin. The boy tries not to hesitate,
reaching out and taking the tail in his smooth palm.
But the thing jerks and writhes, a snake that's been
skinned alive. The boy yells, letting go of it, leaping

backwards and falling hard on his ass, smearing
his way across a slick black pool of animal blood, piss,
and shit on the floor, finally coming to a stop beside
the twitching tail amid a laughing circle of bloody gods.

I. Working with What We Have

Pinkie and the Lions

Neighborhood rooftops fan outward like a mosaic
grouted with city sounds and smells singeing up over
tar paper patches and scorched terra cotta tiles,

aromas of boulevard burger joints and taco shops,
with exhaust fumes from busses, and truck rhythms
rumbling—hissing breaks, groaning gears.

Lying back on the hard hot slope of the roof with Pinkie,
the child's pet dove, nested as if into the shallow well
at the center of her sternum, a fight erupts—her parents

in her house below. The neighbor smokes a cigarette
and walks along his driveway, close to their kitchen
window, calling to his wife so she can can listen too

—the child squints into the eternities of little pinkie's
eyes and the heavens. Meanwhile, mirage beasts arrive
unfurling in red-orange blazes all around them.

Some days she leaps down to her bike and pedals north
to clean mountain breezes, or west to the fresh ocean mist.
More often, lying on her back on that hard hot slope,

she waits—lonely, impatient, watching and listening…
present to an increasingly familiar muse
in the wide orange domes of a flightless dove's eyes,

in red lions rising from a melting rooftop labyrinth
on a carousel of fire sashes billowing towards the sky

I. Working with What We Have

Bar Tender

But at the bar he tends
where they stick dollars
to the ceiling for thirsty souls
who can't pay, he appears

to resent all artists—especially
the authors. More discouraged
than disgruntled, he feels himself
bristling over the dismal mess

he keeps shitting of his life,
who once owned an ebony
fountain pen and an ox-blood
leather satchel. He stares out

through narrow shutter slats
beneath the soiled Lincolns,
who once tended dreams
of being Faulkner.

I. Working with What We Have

Young Ms. Torrez

Young Ms. Torrez taught us how to farm…
with emus here, llamas there, tractors, sheep,
and a hitch in her step where a side-kicking cow
grazed her knee at the fair. How patient she was
with cattle and with us.

Young Ms. Torrez raised goats with her dad
on a farm in the San Joaquin Valley. She also had
a Zebu pair here, Shetland ponies there, strong
knowing arms for the calvings, and good
cowman's sense to soften the sad things.

Torrez said, "A critter won't walk up and tell you
if it's sick or in pain, because predators are great
at picking out the weak and injured in the wild.
So you've got to pay attention, use your instincts,
and figure things out."

Young Ms. Torrez taught us how to castrate
spring lambs. After, when one of the girls asked
why one of the lambs was walking so funny,
Torrez took her aside and gently suggested,
"Why don't you ask one of the guys?"

I. Working with What We Have

Bennies

"We're in the money," he hummed when he got the union job milling birch rails, walnut panels, purple heart, and red oak moldings for millionaire mantels. He taught his sons by example, rarely missing work. Though there was a half-day once, after one of the knives broke. A chunk of steel flew out of his machine, pinging like a round before ricocheting into his meaty breast, dropping him to his knees.

When he went to the office to tape it up, the foreman saw the blood and said, "Better let the doc have a look at that."

"I don't have time. I'm in the middle of a run."

But the foreman made him go. They cleaned him up and started stitching. Then the needle hit something hard and metallic. Through the muscle of his beefy chest, imbedded in the sternum, they found and removed an inch-long, quarter-inch-thick hunk of the broken blade, and sent him home with it. His sons named it *the bullet*, and put it on a key-chain "for good luck." The next day he went back to finish his run.

A year or two later, when two guys ambushed him outside the bar, smashing a kidney and busting his ribs, leaving him on the sidewalk with boot prints, even the nail-marks, kicked into his breast and side, the workday was lost on a trip to Urgent Care. "In the old days, before I had kids, I never would have let anyone stomp me like that," he muttered to the doc.

"My own stupid fault," he said to his sons the next morning, wincing when he coughed, and wearing the brace under his work clothes. "When you have a family, if you're lucky enough to get a union job, you do whatever you have to do to hold onto it. You can't be missing work because you're sick or you got hurt. There are good benefits—and you have to keep them." He drank the last of his coffee before heading out to work.

"It's a great disadvantage in a fight though."

I. Working with What We Have

Beautiful Japanese Quails

They scream in her ear when she drops the broom,
when she reaches down, her head by their enclosures,
to retrieve it. The cages are too small for three hens
and a male—blood smearing with excrement, food,
and feathers, all sticking to everything. She harvests

two-to-six eggs per group. The male tears out feathers
on the back of their heads and the back of their
necks, forcing and forcing his way in, so they bleed
from below their tail feathers too. Some he scalps.
They limp about blinded, blood and bone for a caul.

They scream in her ears. She separates out
the most violent males. But someone else always
returns them. Sometimes when she reaches in,
the females are serene and he is dead, beak open
in a muted scream, eyes gouged in, prepuce engorged

and ravaged, bits of his blood on their beaks and
breast feathers. She lifts him out, makes sure he isn't
breathing, so there's no need to euthanize him, wraps
him in plastic. Then she opens the carcass freezer
setting him beside the dead hens he savaged before.

I. Working with What We Have

Thirst like This

Descending glassy hematite cliffs
the great white ram fronts a pilgrimage
for tart elderberries
dotting the base
of the cavern wall,

leading dams and kids
in nun-like procession, down
from cathedral heights with care
to eat, to savor...
Then with mindful steps

he guides their return, back up
to the ridge of safety.
With the ardor and devotion
of consecrated novices they arrive,
thirsting for this bitter-sweetness.

Nourished, if not sated,
like silent monks they soon depart,
sustained
beneath each lifted heel
by the lotus opening again and again

II. Sketches Near and Far

Tigers of Her Imagination
Chiang Mai, Thailand

The first tiger
was a vegetarian
who bathed
in the Yin River
of the Jolly Mama
and lapped
the foamy custard
of milky coconuts
from open shells
like ice cream cones

until the second
tiger came,
the Yang Marauder,
to split her heart
and strip her bones,
leaving her
with hunger only
blood and meat
could scarcely
pacify or atone.

II. Sketches Near and Far

Flying Dreams
    Maravilla, Los Angeles

"Lean into me
and I'll learn with you,"
his wordless offer
when I was firstborn

who once showed me clouds,
soaring stallions, thunder-kings
on mountain thrones, and lions
roaring across a parched eternity.

Years recently,
only cartoon faces and miniature lambs
in random morsels of popped corn
by a dim light at his kitchen table.

His world has grown so small
who once chased it wide as the sky
where no one could follow him
hanging from the edge

of a cliff above the reservoir
is now clinging
to the tip of this syringe
where I feed him

the chemistry
of hospice,
hoping his dreams
are soft as his sighs

as the fading edges
of his old work scars
where each wound caresses
my brothers' names and mine.

II. Sketches Near and Far

Dolphin Skeleton

> *for Eva Saulitis, renowned scientist and poet, in memoriam, Kachemak Bay, Alaska*

Must all love stories end in tragedy? Are they all fated before they dawn to rescind their happy endings? Near the last of that spectacular summer, I saw it and knew

it was a strange secretive specimen the poet found on her morning hike along the shores of Kachemak Bay. Placing it on the table before me with inestimable delicacy and care, she told us the fragile exotic thing encircling itself was the fetal skeleton of a dolphin.

Mermaid infant-ribs dovetailed the spine like a feather bracelet. In their intricacy I recalled every miniature rice-paper-thin skeleton my father brought home to me. Sparrows, mice, young mud frog mummies.... Treasured relics, the trophies adorned my shelves, more beautiful than broaches or dolls to me then as now.

How, with a child's hands, did I enfold and place each on my windowsill without crushing one? How have the archer's bow lips of this world kissed the delta rising from her heart? Already, we yearn for things our souls are trying to be strong and delicate enough to contain.

Mornings, coiled around myself, it's clear we're all fated to linger after she leaves, pining for treasures hidden in troves the coming springs will never see again.

II. Sketches Near and Far

Novice at the Cafe
New Brunswick, Canada

The last dollar bills she folded into
the shape of a pocket, and tucked
into that the last coins she left
under her empty plate in a fog
the pallor of a dolphin's belly, before
the coming winter in New Brunswick

where the icy spire of the Church
steeple jammed the clouds above
the rows and rows of windows
she washed overlooking the rectory
with old newspapers and vinegar,
and the yards and yards

of wooden floors she scrubbed
and polished by hand on swollen
nun's knees—those windows and floors
that waited for her return,
and the garden that waited
for her callused palms at the hoe,

and the children of Maliseet neighbor
women and men who waited to sing
to her, holding her hands
in the circle of the clan
that took her into it long before
she boarded the train, that gave her

the small bouquet
of forget-me-nots, aware before
the priest or any of her superiors
could guess, she would not return
to her labor there, not that day
or ever again

II. Sketches Near and Far

Red Baseball Cap
Salem, Massachusetts

Dressed in a pale hospital gown
her delicate skin we'd washed,
the IV removed, the monitor
shut off. Earlier that day

I sang *The Rose* for the last
time while I waited
with her, wondering
if she dreamed she was

five years old again, at the inlet
in the red sailboat, fishing
for smelt and haddock
with her father—or age seven,

there in Salem, her red
baseball cap cocked back
on her head while she rode
her bike, wearing blue jeans

and a boy's T-shirt by the sea
all summer long, and slept
in the chapel pews
of the lonely basements

at the homes of neighbors
where Jesus was
her imaginary friend, who
sat beside her in the pews,

who sat beside her
in the chair by the bed
while I hummed *The Rose*
giving her hand into his.

II. Sketches Near and Far

Catchy Tune
French Quarter, New Orleans

She comes down from the *Now and Later*,
the girl who neither trots nor saunters
across the lobby at the fringes
of the convention trying a bit too hard
to resemble a high-and-mighty
who knows what she wants
and exactly where she's going

in those six-inch alligator stilettoes,
tan linen jacket, black shorts,
big blonde waves sprayed hard and stiff
as the gold cardboard crowns
on the king cakes
at Jeanine's Bakery,
and her retro Jackie-O shades.

Perhaps she'll meet up with her aunts
at church some one of these days,
when her back is to the wall
and it's finally high time
for her come-to-Jesus altar call.
Then, she might bow humbly
before her Maker and be slain again

in the spirit. For now, she mugs a wink
at the concierge, making up a new tune
in her head, *But on the eighth day*
God departed and I stumbled
into my treasure,
when that ol' French Quarter
stole my soul in New Orleans.

Yes, on the eighth day, on the eighth day,
on the eighth day God departed...

II. Sketches Near and Far

Michael Callahan, Crab Fisherman
County Kerry, Ireland

In a small skiff he sails out from Ballydavid Bay,
past the cliffs overlooking the Three Sisters
where lichens, mosses, mushrooms, and snails
make a carpet of morsels for rodents, birds, and
black-faced sheep leaping over the fences.

When the winds are up and the waves have their
white ponies on them, Michael Callahan stays
well away from the rocks and doesn't go too far out
of the bay, only far enough to drop in his baskets.
Then he looks up to notice who could be hiking

along the grassy cliffs like a spirit above him.
If it's Sheelah's daughter, from the inn
at the crossroads, she'll wave. And she might
call down, inviting him up for fresh baked scones
with her mother's marmalade and hot black tea.

III. Drawing from Inspiration

Dawn

Ice crystals crackle
thawing while I wait.

Through fanlike eaves
young maples at dawn

she emerges, a whisper,

her padded hooves toeing
the frost-coated underbrush
carpeting a small glen
between us.

Approaching a stream

she lowers her head
sipping without a sound,
ears perked, muscles like ribbons
in a soundless breeze—

yards away, something snaps.

She raises her head
looking towards it,
beads and pearls
falling from her mouth,

then turns to gaze at me.

Ribbons swirl like a cape of cords
as she hurtles herself
around and upwards
while I stand clinging

to rope-like images,

III. Drawing from Inspiration

her back and flanks climbing
in switchback leaps
through long daybreak shadows of trees
lashing the terrain.

Her strength explodes, fire-tongues

lunging skyward
in sunlight traversing
then cresting the mountain
where with one final surge, and the sun

bursting, blazing, at last she is gone.

III. Drawing from Inspiration

Mantis

A large, cream colored mantis
captured me today,
by a wisp of my hair
near the nape of my neck. Not

realizing what had found me,
I flitted it like a leaf that fell
from a limb of the aspen tree
above me while I sat reading.

Unfazed by my flitting,
it regrouped to catch me again
by the bridge of my glasses.
This was no common bug, all but

commanding, "*Look!*" But I flitted
again, so it dropped to my shirt
—a mystical pin to captivate me
with its praying hands

and heart shaped head,
with its cream colored body,
rocking me from sleep, with its
boldness and its poise.

III. Drawing from Inspiration

Coyotl

The first coyote stalked
our new puppy with me.
You waved from the hillock
and we turned back.
When we reached you,
you pointed to the trees.
There, at the mouth
of the clearing she stood,
watching our pup and me.

The second trickster
crouched behind the deer
that trailed down from
the mountains soundlessly
feeding on sweet grasses
and berries by the creek.
It hunted all those rabbits
the gentle deer hadn't meant
to roust and reveal.

Several others arrived
crouching through the years,
ravaging something
dark and mysterious
that once swam or flew.
Still more of them hid unseen
in the off-trail chaparral
barking and howling…
until the last Coyotl gazed

from the embankment beside
the ravine, shoulders knotted
thick with muscles and hide.
She squared off, staring
into my eyes. I took her
into me, leaving
the cavern,
crossing the desert,
carrying them with me.

III. Drawing from Inspiration

Peaches at the Side Yards

The bright yellow hibiscus
by your bedroom window
that also survived the internment
camp, with honeyed apricot trees
and agapanthus from Hawaii
bluing the driveway.

Layers of bandages you unwound
from 'round your bowed swollen
knees while we rested in the shade
at our side yards.
Meanwhile, I threaded needles
for your mending.

How hard you jostled me
slapping my back, nudging me
while we laughed our frequent
wordless conversations to arrive
at a care-full language of smiles,
gestures, and twice we fought tears,

to vanquish my nightmares and soothe
your wounds, some of those contained
in memories and mysteries spanning
generations and histories—your
eighty-four years so many
and my little nine so few.

Before you left, you taught me
with a long rusted nail
spiked into the base
of a Babcock tree
how the peaches came so sweet
in your love-ly garden.

III. Drawing from Inspiration

Golden

Mercy eyes the bakery's flour dusted window. A vendor
emerges—white hair, rusty iguana tinted skin. He struggles
behind a cart brimming with small loaves and colorful sweets.

Mercy watches him until a filthy Chevy distracts her, spinning
'round the corner, tipping something up from the ground—
a flattened sphere, flipped on its edge to roll like a hubcap.

Mercy races a mange crusted mongrel for the spinning disc.
Inches from the dog's canines, she snatches it, still rolling,
to confirm what she hopes: She's won a hardened corn tortilla.

Mercy breaks off a piece, flicking it to her rival. Then
she brushes at the prize and cracks into it with her teeth
—crunching, not really chewing, like trying to eat sand.

Mercy recalls selling her art with that girl from Oaxaca.
And before that, the giant avocados on the southern tip of
the Yucatan that grew so enormous they fell from the trees

splitting open on the ground in rich splendid mounds
like warm butter oozing, glistening fat and golden beneath
the maize-colored disc of the shimmering Mexican sun.

III. Drawing from Inspiration

Cigarettes

I drove Patricia to her chemo appointment that day. It was like any chemo day, until we both saw Amy at the bus stop by the corner. She was puffing away. *She does phlebotomies at a cancer treatment hospital and smokes?* It must have been spackled all over our faces. The girl had been our favorite, so skilled with my beloved's small, rolling veins and hyper-sensitivity to pain.

Patricia sat up sentinel-straight on the passenger side of the front seat. She swiveled her head to stare through her window while we skimmed past. Then Pat turned to me and all but hissed, "I don't *believe* it!" striking her forehead with the heel of her hand. I could hear her rings. Pat repeated the words, raising her hand for another hit. I gripped her wrist while I drove.

Pat shrugged away from my grasp. She straightened her cap then her jacket. "She must know," said Pat, who didn't have to finish it. *She, of all people, must know, working here, of all places, what she's doing to herself. What it's going to do to her family, to anyone who loves her.*

After Pat's treatment, she wanted tea, and I needed coffee. We drove to our favorite cafe.

In the parking lot, cruising for a place to park, Pat grabbed my sleeve. "Pull in, *right there.*" She motioned for me to circle around towards an empty space. It was next to an older model car. Inside the car a man sat smoking a cigarette. Smoke wafted out from his open window. "Right *there,*" Pat repeated. I might have chosen a less toxic spot. But a rare yet familiar edge to Patricia's voice, and the way she gripped my sleeve, underscored how determined she could be. Her foot was down and it wasn't coming up again.

So, I parked to the smoker's left where Pat's window was directly opposite and closest to his. When I shut off the engine he looked over and gave us a neighborly smile. Pat sat up as tall as she could, given her petite frame. She faced him. He smiled again. She ripped off her cap and jutted her face, neck, and shoulders out of the window. If she could, I'm sure she meant to singe him with her baldness and her pallor.

III. Drawing from Inspiration

He rolled up his window, still looking at her, then at me, nodding, as if to assure us, her, *It's okay. I get it. I know you're not well. And I won't let any of my smoke reach...* But Pat continued to glare at him. I can only assume it was a boring through, from the way she sat, bolted to her spot with both hands clasping the rim of her door, head reaching as far out of the window as she could crane her neck and shoulders. She said no word, uttered no sound.

The man continued to look at Pat. Then, as if finally seeing her, his expression changed. It became that of a child in pain, and of the child's father suffering with her, both of them startled by the child's discovery in the woods, of a small perfect creature shot vermilion.

Then he turned away, toward the console of his old car, and mashed out the cigarette.

III. Drawing from Inspiration

Late in the Dawning

On a courtyard bench she dreams
with her eyes half-open again.
Bee murmurings wake her
from azalea blossoms so fragile

they bruise if bee-bustled too hard.
Meanwhile, a giant Japanese beetle
with metallic green wings for armor
whirs by tank like and thunks

down on the concrete—dead.
Granite planes bisect the ancient
meadows hidden beneath
this modern labyrinth.

There's cold wind and layers of her life
in alchemy fructifying gifts
from the catacombs. Already a cornucopia,
even with shock and loss still stinging,

if less intensely, back of her neck
to the base of her spine,
and her core still sore from the thrashing.
Any luck, this heart will soon,

relatively speaking, be broken again
she pretends not to know
as busy, brilliant children and ancients
buzz and hustle by

imagining, believing
there's no time to waste,
no space to attend
to inexplicable beauty even she

sometimes fails to taste
while eating, while it's already
so late…so very late
in the dawning.

IV. Gaining Perspective

Lucky

He gives his dogs names,
like *Hope*
and *Lucky*.
"Lucky! Lucky! Lucky!
Come here!"

He has a hound named
Courage. Mornings,
he calls him long
and loud, for anyone
who needs to hear.

With Courage and Hope
he goes down to the docks
where his town dips off
towards the sea.
At a grill by the harbor

he shares coffee and toast
with anyone there
between jobs, between
homes, watching, waiting,
"Hope! Hope!" hoping.

IV. Gaining Perspective

Superhero

But no matter how
many times they foisted
the roles of Wonder Woman
and Hawkgirl upon her,
foisting her onto the roles,

she wanted to be Mother
Theresa before anyone
outside of Calcutta knew
what she was doing,
and Saint Francis

when he was still listening
to the noisy doves instead of
telling said doves
what to do. For two full cycles
of seasons, she tried

to find her place among them,
the fighting priests and priestesses
under the mantels they imposed.
But it wasn't until after
she went away—forty days

that lasted for years—and returned
to discover they still fought
among themselves
over the same super-issues
with the same non-outcomes.

That's when she understood
the healing she might channel.
Predictably, though, she knew
they only wanted her to be
the hero they wanted.

IV. Gaining Perspective

Gifted

When the sun tips its apex
she leaves work
to toe a velvet footpath.
Roses and camellias are heirlooms

in this near-perfect world
where even Schweitzers
and Curies rested sometimes.
She prizes these half hours.

Others come and go
transient as sunlight flecking
bits of gold-leaf
through dark moving patterns

in the hovering oaks.
On sharp borders
they pass. She sees their footprints
and their ancestors' marking

right-angles and rare diagonals
across the perpendicular geometry
of this jeweled terrain.
From a world in every mind

some have come to seek
the whispered greetings in her eyes
with theirs that glance at her
then downward. There is

—palpable as homesickness or grief,
if mild as the air between them—
a longing for things they can't name
any more than she could at their age

even amid all this exactitude,
perhaps because of it.
In spite of it, she sees abstractions
like wealth and transformation

IV. Gaining Perspective

lying pupate within them...

and
wonders if
they recognize her too

from places they have yet

to see, if time is not
linear after
all.

Holding a half-eaten pear
she sips tepid tomato juice
from a small metal-tasting can
remembering the earth's hot cider

on crisp mountain mornings and
groves of apple trees stippled with dew.
There, a young woman strums
a bluesy steel guitar while

chimney smoke spices the canyon.
The sunrise sky is Neptune-blue
as her beloved's eyes
at high, high tide

and the ocean comes up daily
in fullness and perfection
as if for no reason but
to engulf these mountains.

*Will you ever, can you begin
to imagine?* She wants to ask them,
the gifted minds, the shy young hearts
passing her by.

IV. Gaining Perspective

Like Father, like Daughter

At age seven, he watches
    the hooky-cop drive away while his
mother calls out from their porch
    at the rim of the reservoir, throwing
down her dishcloth like a gauntlet.

Since the boy is going
    to get another beating, regardless,
he returns to the cattail thickets
    for hours, braving tarantulas,
bobcats, and the occasional

Abel Borracho, escaped
    from County Jail.
When he finally comes home,
    in desperation Josepha breaks
wooden hangers on her son's head

then throws him in the cellar, and
    much as the woman wants,
rarely shows him any affection.
    At seven, rats in the dark
are worse to him than bobcats or welts.

Later, no surprise, unlike Pip,
    he will have dogs, guns, knives
and a chip on his shoulder
    big as Sisyphus' boulder to push
uphill for the rest of his life.

As a young man, he gets fired
    for shutting the mouth
of the foreman's son—
    shoving him up against a wall
with a forearm under his chin

IV. Gaining Perspective

and a crowbar cocked
    to crack his skull. "Mom,"
he asks years later, after they
    survive all this, when his mother
and others depend upon him,

"how come
    you never smiled
or played with me
    when I was
a kid?"

"You were bad enough
    as it was," Josepha tells him.
"Can you imagine
    what would have happened
if I did?"

At age seven, overhearing,
    his daughter   can   imagine,
and wishes they had been children
    together, she and her father, safe
in the reservoir all through the years.

IV. Gaining Perspective

Before the Ecstasy

The tall pale
man at the bar
who watches
the bartender brim
his drink,

who rolls up his
sleeves, loosing
his tie and closing
his eyes before taking
the first lingering sip,

who hunkers down
over the cocktail like
someone leaning over
the palmed enchanted
fruit from the tree

of knowledge
to relish the first
forbidden bite.
The bartender is
a gentleman

leaving him to it,
moving to the other
end of the bar
—for the protocol
and intimacy

of the moment
require this—
    reminding me of my
first grade teacher,
Mrs. Kai, who,

    discovering me alone
again in the Rowan Avenue
Elementary School

IV. Gaining Perspective

Library
pouring over

mildewed volumes
of fairy tales
and fables,
the occasional
epitaph collection

and especially
all poetry,
   tiptoed away
on petite quiet feet,
leaving me to them.

In the garden,
I never paused for Adam
or for permission
   drinking fully,
copious rivers of ecstasy.

IV. Gaining Perspective

Petals

Every now and again
I meet her on the trail

whose smile reminds me
of the pale pink petals

that hue and silk the ground
beneath azaleas after it rains.

Many years from now, when
I'm still nowhere happier

than out on the trails,
if I smile

and another sees azalea
petals fading,

let me finally
still be rejoicing

This page is for capturing images, conversations, and inspirations
from your home or around your neighborhood,
at the
park
or in
a pub,
even at
the library,
perhaps seated at table, right
where you are, watching, listening, paying attention.

California poet **Diane Solis** was born in Los Angeles, earned her BA and teaching credentials from Loyola Marymount University, and resides on the Central Pacific Coast with her life partner. Diane's poetry has been nominated for a Pushcart Prize, excerpted in *Expressive Writing: Classroom and Community*, and has been published or is forthcoming in numerous literary journals and magazines, including, *America—The Jesuit Review, Psychological Perspectives: Quarterly Journal of Jungian Thought*, and *The Healing Muse—Annual Journal of the Center for Ethics and Humanities at SUNY*.

Teacher, science writer, and technical editor by trades, Solis has practiced yoga since she was a child and contemplative meditation since she was in high school. In 2005 her partner and love of her life of eight years died suddenly and at a young age after fighting off cancer. With the new love of her life of ten years, Diane travels near and far to photograph, paint, and write chiefly about the natural world, especially the "wild" she encounters there.
dianesolisarts@gmail.com